YOUR LAND
AND
MY LAND
AFRICA

We Visit

NIGERIA

Karen Bush

Gibson

Mitchell Lane
PUBLISHERS

P.O. Box 196
Hockessin, Delaware 19707

YOUR LAND
AND
MY LAND
AFRICA

Egypt
Ethiopia
Ghana
Kenya
Libya
Madagascar
Morocco
Nigeria
Rwanda
South Africa

IBYA

EGYPT

Aswān

YOUR LAND
AND
MY LAND
AFRICA

We Visit

NIGERIA

SUDAN

Gulf of Aden

Addis
Ababa

Copyright © 2013 by Mitchell Lane Publishers, Inc. All rights reserved. No part of this book may be reproduced without written permission from the publisher. Printed and bound in the United States of America.

Printing   1   2   3   4   5   6   7   8   9

Library of Congress Cataloging-in-Publication Data
Gibson, Karen Bush.
We visit Nigeria / by Karen Gibson.
        p. cm. — (Your land and my land. Africa)
Includes bibliographical references and index.
ISBN 978-1-61228-309-8 (library bound)
1. Nigeria—Juvenile literature. I. Title. II. Series: Your land and my land (Mitchell Lane Publishers). Africa.
DT515.22.G53 2013
966.9—dc23

                                                       2012041973

eBook ISBN: 9281612283838

PUBLISHER'S NOTE: This story is based on the author's extensive research, which she believes to be accurate. Documentation of this research is on page 60.

   The internet sites referenced herein were active as of the publication date. Due to the fleeting nature of some websites, we cannot guarantee they will all be active when you are reading this book.

                                                               PLB

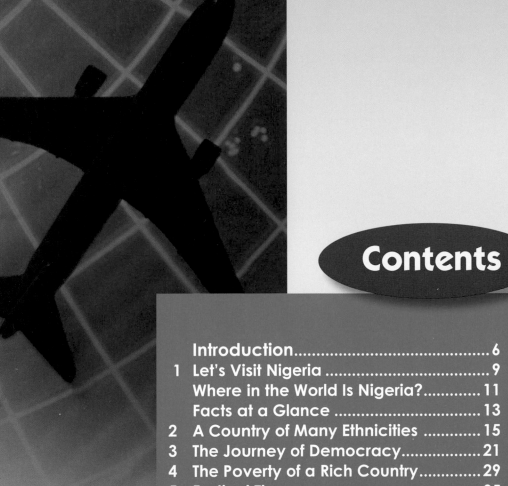

Contents

Introduction

Sannu! That means "Hello!" in the Hausa language from the West African country of Nigeria. Nigeria is one of fifty-seven countries that make up Africa, the second-largest continent in the world after Asia. Africa is a continent of deserts and rainforests, grasslands and forests, and mountains and beaches.

People think of many things when they think about Africa—wild animals, jungles, hunger, and wars. But Africa is much more than that.

Scientists know that human life began in Africa. About five million years ago, human ancestors called hominids lived in Africa's grasslands and forests. In 1974, the partial skeleton of a hominid was discovered in the African country of Ethiopia. Known as Lucy, she is more than three million years old. Lucy has taught scientists much about early pre-human life.

About 1.8 million years ago, early humans decided to see what else the world held. They moved from Africa to Asia because this was the only place they could reach by foot. There were no boats or airplanes for travel. Once in Asia, some continued moving further east into that continent. Others turned west towards Europe. The entire human population of today's world originated in Africa.

Abeokuta, Nigeria

NIGERIA

AFRICA

With over 170 million people, Nigeria is Africa's most populated country. In fact, one out of every six Africans is Nigerian. Nigeria is also the eighth-most populated country in the world, but it isn't Africa's largest country. Fourteenth in size, Nigeria is about the size of California, Arizona, and Nevada combined. Nigeria can seem very crowded, but most of the crowding is in the cities.

Nigeria is located on the west coast of Africa near the equator. As part of the sub-Saharan region of Africa, Nigeria is a lot like the entire African continent—the geography changes as you travel across the country.

Bordering the Atlantic Ocean at the Gulf of Guinea, Nigeria also borders the African countries of Niger, Cameroon, Benin, and Chad. Both Nigeria and Niger get their name from the Niger River, the third-longest river in Africa after the Nile and the Congo.

Like the rest of Africa, Nigeria is a country of variety. The land and the people have many differences, but together, they are Nigerian. Let's visit Nigeria.

During an Igbo Masquerade Festival, masqueraders are covered from head to toe in costumes and masks made of cloth, straw, or wood.

Let's Visit Nigeria

Costumed from head to foot, masqueraders dance to songs played by the *oja,* a native flute, and drums. Hand-held percussion instruments add to the beat. If you listen carefully, you can hear the sounds of bells. Look closely and you'll find the bells decorating some of the costumes. Although many costumes shine with bright colors and all have masks, no two costumes are alike.

Masqueraders are people who wear masks made from wood or straw. They tell stories with their movements and their appearance. Dance troupes, also in native costumes, dance for the crowds. Welcome to an Igbo Masquerade Festival.

The Igbo are one of the three main ethnic groups of Nigeria. Most Igbo live in southern Nigeria. Their very long cultural history includes masking or masquerading. The people in colorful robes and masks might represent an ancestor or perhaps symbolize an animal such an elephant, crocodile, or snake.

In Enugu, one of thirty-six states in Nigeria, the Council of Arts and Culture holds the Enugu State Mmanwu (Masquerade) Festival each November. The city where the festival is held is also named Enugu and is the capital of the state. The festival begins with a masquerade parade. Everyone's costume is so complete that you wouldn't be able to recognize a dancer unless you knew his costume. Thousands of Nigerians and a few tourists watch the parade of masked dancers move through the streets.

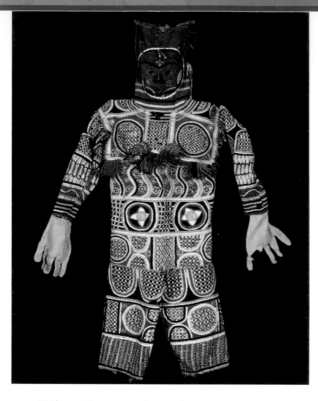

One the best-known Igbo costumes is the *Agbogho Mmuo,* or Maiden-Mother Spirit. The costume represents the beauty of both a young maiden spirit and her mother.

When the parade ends, everyone moves to a large stadium. In other festivals held in smaller villages, the stage might be a large, open space. In Enugu, the stadium is a modern location that works well for larger audiences.

The crowd in the stadium's seats is filled with excitement. Suddenly, all is quiet. The sound of flute music begins to float softly in the air. A drum joins in and anticipation builds. A single masked dancer enters the stadium. His costume is brilliant with colors that capture the sunlight. Other masqueraders, all men, follow. Someone appears in an eagle masquerade, and the crowd gasps. The eagle is very important

FYI FACT:

The Afikpo Igbo are members of the Igbo cultural group who live in the eastern region. They have a traditional belief that good luck is fate, but that you can catch bad luck from someone else.

WHERE IN THE WORLD IS NIGERIA?

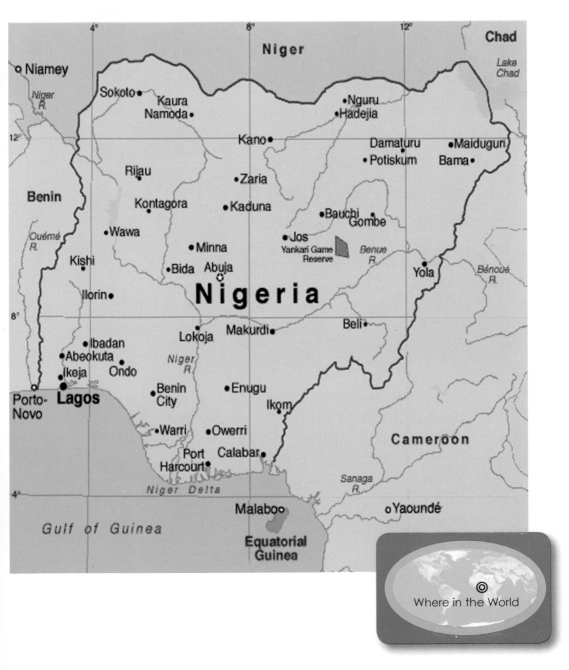

Where in the World

The Igbo have long lived in villages like this one. In many villages, a council represents the community in political matters with the government.

to the Igbo, symbolizing strength and purity. In villages, senior men were once awarded eagle feathers to indicate their high status.

The masked people dance. Several dance groups also take turns dancing. Although the masqueraders are men, many members of the dance groups are women. Each group wears a different costume. Soon, everyone is dancing. Boys and young men slip past security and join the dancing on the stadium floor.

Organizations like the Council of Arts and Culture and the government realize that it's important for the people of Nigeria to have pride in their culture and their country. Events like the Mmanwu Festival help people forget their disagreements and celebrate the Nigerian culture that they share.

NIGERIA FACTS AT A GLANCE

Nigerian Flag

Full name: Federal Republic of Nigeria

Official language: English (over 500 languages are spoken; the most common include Hausa, Yoruba, Igbo, and Fulani)

Population: 170,123,740 (July 2012 estimate)

Land area: 356,668 square miles (923,768 square kilometers); roughly two times the size of California

Capital: Abuja

Government: Federal republic

Ethnic makeup: Over 250 ethnic groups. Primary groups are Hausa and Fulani 29%, Yoruba 21%, Igbo 18%, Ijaw 10%, Kanuri 4%, Ibibio 3.5%, Tiv 2.5%

Religions: Muslim 50%, Christian 40%, indigenous 10%

Exports: petroleum, rubber, cocoa

Imports: food and live animals, machinery, transportation equipment, chemicals, manufactured goods

Crops: peanuts, cocoa, palm oil, cotton, yams

Average high temperatures:
   Lagos: February 91°F (33°C); August 82°F (28°C)
   Kano: April 100°F (38°C); August 84°F (29°C)

Average rainfall: ranges from 60-170 inches (152-432 centimeters) on the coast, and from 20-50 inches (50-130 centimeters) inland

Highest point: Chappal Waddi—7,936 feet (2,419 meters) above sea level

Longest river: The Niger River—2,600 miles (4,180 kilometers)

Flag: The Nigerian flag was adopted in 1960 after the country gained independence from Britain. The green represents Nigeria's forests and agriculture, while the white is for unity and peace.

National sport: Soccer (football)

National flower: *Costus spectabilis*

National bird: Black crowned crane

National tree: Camphor tree

Source: *CIA World Factbook:* Nigeria

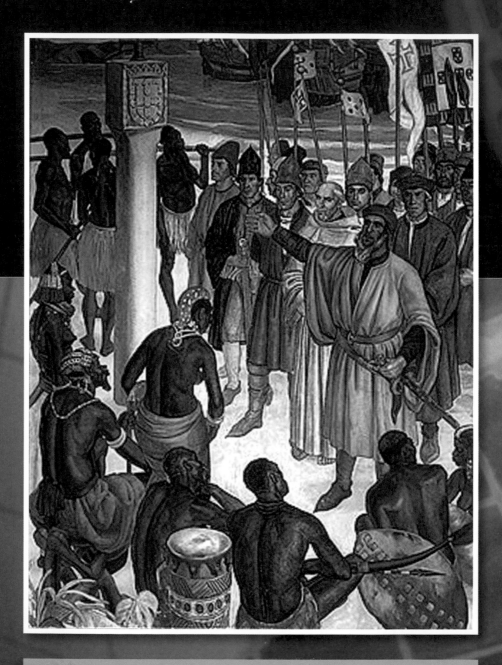

The first Europeans that Nigerian tribes came into contact with were Portuguese traders in the 15th century.

A Country of
Many Ethnicities

The Masquerade Festival is one of many ways the people of Nigeria celebrate their heritage. With over 250 ethnic groups calling Nigeria home, it can be difficult for visitors to understand the differences.

While English is the official language, most Nigerians speak one or two tribal languages too. In fact, a child's first language is often something other than English. These tribal languages are the languages you may hear most often when you travel through Nigeria. With the hundreds of languages spoken by the many ethnic groups, there is no way to know them all. If a Nigerian doesn't know the native language of the person to whom he is speaking, he will speak English. Sometimes the English is a combination of English and words from native languages, known as *Pidgin.* As the official language, English also doesn't show any favoritism to any one ethnic group in Nigeria.

The English language came to Nigeria by way of European colonialism. In the 15th century, European explorers began sailing to Africa —mainly the Portuguese, French, Dutch, and the British. These countries all began to claim certain areas of the African continent as colonies of their countries. Europe did the same when they came to North America. The American colonies fought a war—the American Revolution—to become an independent country.

Many of the Europeans who first came to Africa were traders. Some of the first items Europeans wanted to trade were people. The

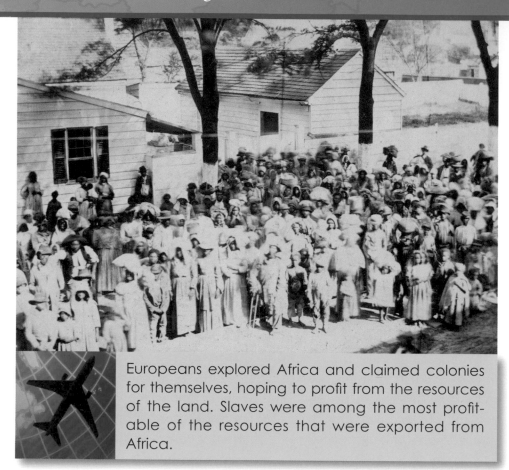

Europeans explored Africa and claimed colonies for themselves, hoping to profit from the resources of the land. Slaves were among the most profitable of the resources that were exported from Africa.

Portuguese were the first Europeans in Nigeria. They gave the port city of Lagos its name, which means "lakes" in Portuguese. Coastal ports such as Lagos were used to ship captured Africans to work as slaves on plantations in the Caribbean and the Americas. After the United States won its independence, it too participated in the slave trade.

In the 19th century, the slave trade was largely replaced by trading commodities. In Nigeria, those commodities were palm oil and timber. The British banned the slave trade in 1807, and used its military power to stop other countries who were attempting to trade slaves. The Royal British Navy patrolled the West African coast to monitor the ban, and freed Africans who were being transported as slaves.

By 1861, Lagos was officially ruled by the British. From that time, British interest in Nigeria spread. In 1886, the Royal Niger Company was chartered by the British for the business of trade along the Niger River. The British used these traders to rule indirectly through local kings or by turning different ethnic groups against each other. By 1900, Britain controlled Nigeria. It was made formal in 1914 when the area became known as the Colony and Protectorate of Nigeria.

Nigerians in the North, mostly Hausa, had an indirect rule agreement with the British. This meant that the leaders, usually the religious leaders, had some voice in how things operated. Life in northern Nigeria remained more traditional. Most were Muslim, so daily and religious life was quite different than it was for the Christian Igbo, the chief ethnic group in the southeast. The Yoruba, the dominant people in the southwest, were evenly divided between Islam and Christianity. In the South, British customs and education influenced native Nigerians. These differences can still be seen today.

Relationships between the different ethnic groups and religions have a long and violent history. Countless Nigerians have died because of their ethnic background or religion. Christians and Muslims still have disagreements. Fighting between the Hausa and Yoruba is common as well. In the North, many Muslim states have enacted Islamic law, called shari'a. This upsets the Christian populations who don't have the same values.

The Hausa, Igbo, and Yoruba ethnic groups make up about 60 percent of Nigeria's population. Another 10 percent of Nigerians are Fulani, who are sometimes grouped with the Hausa. The remainder of Nigerians are spread among smaller ethnic groups who follow indigenous religions and beliefs. There are both Muslims and Christians who still follow indigenous practices as well.

A Nigerian's ethnic group is very important to him or her. For many people, it's more important than being Nigerian or African. Nigerian author Chinua Achebe addressed this in his first novel, *Things Fall Apart,* published in 1958. *Things Fall Apart* is considered one of the most important books to ever come out of Africa. It has been translated into fifty languages.

Achebe's famous novel is set in the late 19th century. The protagonist is Okonkwo, a respected leader in his Igbo village. He takes in a boy, Ikemefuna, who has been captured by the village. Living with the family, Ikemefuna looks to Okonkwo as a father. But when the elders insist that the boy be killed, Okonkwo joins others in beating the boy to death. After this event, Okonkwo's life becomes a series of bad events. He is sent away for several years, and returns to find a very different village. White missionaries have come, changing the government and religion. Okonkwo begins to fight for the traditional way of life, but finds that the rest of the village is not behind him.

Born in southeastern Nigeria on November 16, 1930, Chinua Achebe was the fifth of six children from an Igbo Christian family. His name at birth was Albert Chinualumogu Achebe. He was named after the husband of Britain's Queen Victoria, Prince Albert. Proud of his Nigerian heritage, Achebe gave up the British name "Albert" while in college.

Nigerian writer Chinua Achebe is often called the father of modern African literature. A novelist and poet, he has received approximately twenty-five honorary doctorates from universities throughout the world.

Chinua Achebe (left) and South Africa's Nelson Mandela have been important activists for the rights of native Africans.

After graduating from college, Achebe worked briefly as a teacher, and then for the Nigerian Broadcasting Service. During this time, he began writing *Things Fall Apart*. He disliked how Africans were represented in the books about Africa by foreign writers, and he wanted to change this.

Achebe became politically active, writing and speaking about the problems of the Igbo. He also supported and encouraged young African writers. In 1972, Achebe came to the United States to teach English at the University of Massachusetts and later the University of Connecticut. He returned to Nigeria in 1976 and continued to write. After the publication of *Anthills of the Savanna* in 1987, he taught at several United States universities.

Back home in Nigeria in 1990, Achebe was in a car accident. His injuries led to paralysis from the waist down. Doctors recommended that he receive medical care in the U.S., so he returned a third time to teach at Bard College in New York and receive medical attention.

Achebe has written and published novels, children's books, short stories, essays, and poems. His village of Ogidi honored him in 1999 for his books about Nigerian myths and legends.

After the country gained independence, Nigerian leaders were recognized around the world. Here, American jazz legend Louis Armstrong meets the Premier of Northern Nigeria, Sir Ahmadu Bello.

Chapter 3

The Journey of Democracy

The fighting and arguing between Nigeria's ethnic groups has a long history. It seemed to grow worse after Nigeria won its independence in 1960. Everyone had an idea about how the country should be run.

In October 1960, Nigeria adopted a constitution for a parliamentary type of federal government similar to Britain's. The federal government would be in charge of defense, foreign relations, and economic policies. Nigeria's three regions—North, West, and East—were allowed to govern themselves in other matters. The regions were similar to the three sections that the Niger and Benue rivers divide the country into. Each region was also largely populated by one of the three main ethnic groups.

In 1963, Nigeria declared itself a federal republic with a new constitution and a fourth region, the Midwest. A federal republic has a constitution and states, like the United States. Still, people disagreed about how the government should be run. In 1966, Igbo army officers staged a coup and later took over the government with General Johnson Aguiyi-Ironsi as the head of state. The Igbo government didn't last long, about five months.

Afterward, the ruling military took over and divided the four regions into twelve states. Again, the constitution was revised. The Igbo didn't like the changes and seceded from the rest of Nigeria, just like the Southern United States seceded from the Union before the U.S. Civil War.

The Igbo called their new country the Republic of Biafra after a nearby bay. Colonel Chukwuemeka Odumegwu Ojukwu, educated in England, became president.

A federal Nigerian soldier ready with his anti-tank bazooka during the Nigerian Civil War

Civil war broke out in 1967. For three years, Nigerians fought against each other. Nigeria kept food and supplies from the Igbo states with the Biafra blockade. Over one million Igbo people died, mainly from starvation. Soon after the capture of the Biafran towns of Owerri and Uli in 1970, the Igbo surrendered and the Republic of Biafra was dissolved. Nigeria's head of state, General Yakubu Gowon, offered amnesty to all whom submitted to federal authority.

It was a sad time for Nigeria, as the war had caused the deaths of so many people. Most Nigerians don't want another civil war, so they try to get along. But the ethnic and geographical divisions generally continue today. The differences are strongest between the North and the South, where it can seem as if Nigeria is two different countries.

In the 1970s, continued coups and violence characterized the government. People began to ask for a civilian government, instead of a military one. General Murtala Muhammed became Nigeria's leader in 1975 and promised civilian rule by 1979. Instead, he was assassinated during a Lagos traffic jam in 1976. However, Muhammed's chief of staff, General Olusegun Obasanjo, followed through with Muhammed's plans. Obasanjo created seven more states in 1976.

The Second Republic was born, and in 1977 an elected constituent assembly created a new constitution. Five political parties were established, and elections were held in 1979. The National Assembly, similar to the U.S. Congress, contained people elected from all five political parties. Alhaji Shehu Shagari of the National Party of Nigeria was elected president.

Four years later, Shagari and National Party of Nigeria won the majority of the elections again. Rumors that the voting was rigged led to violent protests. Soon, another military coup overthrew the civilian government.

The Supreme Military Council, headed by Major General Muhammadu Buhari, took control and many freedoms were lost. Buhari lasted less than two years before Major General Ibrahim Babangida overthrew him in 1985. Called "the Redeemer" by many Nigerians, Babangida returned freedom to the press and released political prisoners. He also focused on economic recovery for Nigeria.

A Third Republic was established in 1989 with still another constitution. In early 1990, a group tried and failed to overthrow Babangida. Officials arrested over 200 people believed to have been part of the plot. Many were executed following secret trials.

Elections were again tried in 1990, starting with local and then state elections. The presidential election was postponed until June 12, 1993. Outsiders monitoring the elections said it was the fairest election ever held in Nigeria. When election returns started coming in, it looked like Yoruba businessman M.K.O. Abiola would win the presidency.

Babangida annulled the election, and riots broke out. More than a hundred people were killed before Babangida agreed to hand over power to an interim government that would rule until the 1994 elections. Instead, Defense Minister Sani Abacha took control. He disbanded all democratic political offices and appointed military officers as the heads of states.

Many Nigerians believed that democracy was the path to peace for Nigeria. The National Democratic Coalition (NADECO) was formed to campaign for a democratic civilian government. In May 1994, elections were held for a Constitutional Conference, but Abacha would not allow candidates who opposed him to run. The majority of Nigerians refused to vote in the elections.

Chaos followed as petroleum unions and other workers' unions went on strike to protest. Almost all business halted. An already troubled economy was in even worse shape. Abacha removed the union leaders from office and arrested anyone who opposed him. Human rights activists, journalists, and relatives of anyone who had protested against Abacha were jailed. Some were sentenced to death.

M.K.O. Abiola, the popular democratic leader who ran for president in 1993, and Ken Saro-Wiwa, a writer and environmentalist, were among the many who were arrested. Saro-Wiwa was executed by hanging on November 10, 1995. After these actions, many countries throughout the world, including the United States, announced sanctions against the Nigerian government. Travel was restricted, and the U.S. refused to sell weapons to Nigeria.

Elections were scheduled, but Abacha insisted that all five political parties nominate him as their candidate. Before elections could be held, Abacha died of a heart attack. The Nigerian population celebrated. They hoped that his death would bring the end of the turmoil that had characterized the government for so many years. Young adults who were just reaching the age requirement for voting had never known anything different.

General Abdulsalami Abubakar succeeded Abacha. Military officers in political offices, particularly those appointed by Abacha, were retired or fired. Abubakar began releasing political prisoners. On the night before M.K.O. Abiola was to be released after four years of imprisonment, he died of a heart attack.

Abubakar set up elections through the Independent National Electoral Commission. Local elections were held first in December 1998. The presidential and legislative elections were held three months later. Olusegun Obasanjo, who had introduced civilian rule in the 1970s, was one of the prisoners released by Abubakar. He ran as the People's

FYI FACT:

When Nigeria gained its independence in 1960, women in the South were permitted to vote, but women in the North could not vote until the 1979 elections. Almost 23 percent of the government's ministerial positions were held by women in 2001. By 2004, women also held seats in both the House of Representatives and the Senate.

President Goodluck Jonathan usually dresses in a black caftan shirt, black pants, and a black fedora on his head.

Democratic Party (PDP) presidential candidate and won the 1999 election. Candidates from the PDP also won the majority of the legislative seats.

Along with the 1999 election came a new constitution, although it was very similar to the one passed in 1979. The National Assembly would include a 360-member House of Representatives and 109 elected officials in the Senate. Each of the thirty-six states would have three senators, and the federal capital territory of Abuja would have one senator.

Olusegun Obasanjo was sworn in as president on May 29, 1999. After sixteen years of military rule, Nigeria had a democratic government once again. But it was a democratic government with many problems from past abuses and corruption.

Nigerian President Olusegun Obasanjo (right) is shown here with United States President Jimmy Carter in 1977.

Obasanjo released many people who were being held without charges. He created a panel to investigate human rights violations. His government tried to track down billions of dollars of Nigeria's funds being held in secret overseas bank accounts. Obasanjo formed the National Security Commission in 2001 to address the ongoing ethnic violence. Much of the violence is attributed to conflicts between Muslims and Christians, in addition to disputes between residents and oil companies in the petroleum-rich Niger Delta area.

Things have improved, but it has taken time to work out how the executive, legislative, and judicial branches of government will work together. Also, state governments are sometimes at odds with the federal government in Abuja. President Obasanjo was reelected in 2003 amid the usual rumors of illegal voting procedures.

Nigeria limits presidents to two terms, just as the United States does. Obasanjo could not run for a third term. On April 21, 2007, voters chose from twenty-four candidates in elections filled with problems and illegalities. People who were unhappy with the results protested. Several political parties—All Nigeria People's Party, Progressive Peoples Alliance, and the Action Congress of Nigeria—challenged results in thirty-four out of thirty-six states.

Despite the questionable elections, Nigeria saw a transfer of power between two civilian governments for the first time. Umaru Yar'Adua, a former governor of the state of Katsina, was elected. His election was upheld by Nigeria's Supreme Court 4 to 3.

After two and a half years in office, President Yar'Adua became ill. His vice-president, Goodluck Jonathan, served as acting president in his absence. Six months later, Yar'Adua died, and Jonathan was officially sworn in as president.

In April 2011, Goodluck Jonathan was re-elected with 59 percent of the vote. The People's Democratic Party continues to be the domi-

FYI FACT:

American newspapers and television are readily available in Nigeria. Turn on the television and you're sure to see old reruns of American TV shows.

President Goodluck Jonathan was elected by the people as president of Nigeria after serving as acting president for two years.

nant party, although the Action Congress of Nigeria party has gained seats in the National Assembly and in state governments. Although electoral problems were still noted, most people considered the 2011 election to be the fairest in Nigeria since 1999.

For many people, Goodluck Jonathan seemed to come from out of nowhere, but in reality, his rise to the top office in the country happened over time, without much publicity. His quieter personality differs from many of Nigeria's previous leaders. Born in 1957 to a canoe-making family, Jonathan is from the Ijaw ethnic group in the Niger Delta region. After studying zoology in college, he worked as an environmental protection officer and lecturer.

Jonathan entered politics in 1998. Within a year, he was elected deputy governor in his home state of Bayelsa. When the governor was impeached for corruption, Jonathan filled the position.

The president at that time, Olusegun Obasanjo, asked Jonathan to run for vice-president in 2007. He won and became the number two leader in the country. With the illness of President Yar'Adua, Jonathan became acting president, and then president after Yar'Adua's death.

President Jonathan is a man who works toward making changes, and speaks of supporting all Nigerians. He is also a modern man with a Facebook page and over 800,000 followers. He tells people, "my life has always been about service."[1]

Nigeria seems to be on the right track now after many years of fighting. Nigerians have to work hard to get along with one another, but pride in their country motivates people to move toward peace and unity.

Fishermen make their last catch of the day before the sun gives way to evening along the Niger River.

The Poverty of a Rich Country

In 1956, oil was discovered in Olubiri, a village in the Niger Delta. The delta is an area characterized by swamps, grasslands, and annual flooding. It was formed by the flow of the Niger River through the area. In northwestern Nigeria, the Niger River enters the country and meets the Benue River, flowing from the east. Joined together, the Niger River flows south through tropical rainforests until it reaches the delta. In the delta, the river runs off into streams and swamps before emptying into the Gulf of Guinea in the Atlantic Ocean.

The Niger Delta is the largest delta in Africa. When the 1970s arrived, the country's leaders began to capitalize on an export that other countries wanted—petroleum. Nigeria experienced an oil boom and focused its economy on the export of petroleum. Today, petroleum makes up 95 percent of Nigeria's exports. Cocoa, leather products, and rubber are some of the others.

Depending on a single export is dangerous for a country's economy. Nigeria is dependent on world oil prices, which has led to economic problems for the country. Nigeria's main export partner is the United States. It also exports to the European Union, India, Brazil, and Japan.

Nigeria's agriculture industry hasn't been able to keep up with the growth of its population, so Nigerians import much of their food. What commercial agriculture there is, including fisheries, is poorly managed and not getting the attention it needs to grow successfully.

Most Nigerian farmers have not made use of improvements in farming technology, and don't produce as much food as they could.

Petroleum sells for high prices. Many people in Nigeria expected to make money from it, but only a small percentage have actually been able to. A much larger part of the population has become increasingly poor. In Olubiri, there is no electricity, clean water, or school. Port Harcourt, a city in the middle of the delta, is made up of slums and dangerous gangs. Visitors are asked to be very careful in the Niger Delta, where both homes and people are stolen.

Nigeria's main resource is also dangerous to the land. Pollution and oil spills from the mining of petroleum have endangered the fish in rivers and streams. A large amount of land has been cleared for building—from 1990 to 2010, 49 percent of Nigeria's forests were cut down. Because there are so few left, the forests that remain are that much more important.

Major oil spills occur frequently in the Niger Delta, causing people to become ill and land to be destroyed.

The largest protected area is Gashaka-Gumti National Park, one of eight national parks in Nigeria. It is named after two historic villages in the eastern area of Nigeria, Gashaka and Gumti. The 2,600-square-mile (6,700-square-kilometer) park contains montane forests, sometimes called cloud forests because of the mist and fog. You will find elephants, hippopotamuses, and buffalo grazing in the park's woodland savannas. You might even spot a lion there. Leopards reside in the rainforest, which is also West Africa's most important primate habitat. Here, you will find the "Nigerian chimpanzee," a chimpanzee subspecies found only in Nigeria and neighboring Cameroon. Without protection, it could become extinct within twenty years.

In northeastern Nigeria, Yankari National Park is considered one of West Africa's best game parks. It's only open seven months of the year and requires guides. A large number of wildlife species live in the park, including hippos, lions, monkeys, and warthogs. The park has the largest population of elephants in West Africa, about 500. Located near the park lodge is Wiki Warm Springs, a clear lake often visited by elephants and baboons. Human visitors like swimming in the Wiki Warm Springs, too.

Northern Nigeria is part of Africa's Sahel region. Located south of the Sahara Desert, the Sahel is hot and dry—and not much grows there. Savannas and low hills are found in the central part of Nigeria, while mangrove swamps and streams meander through the delta in the south.

Mountains divide Nigeria from the neighboring country of Cameroon. The highest mountain is Chappal Waddi, rising to 7,936 feet (2,419 meters). It also goes by the name of Gangirwal or "Mountain of Death." Although the terrain is uneven, the mountain seems to get its name instead from a myth that the keeper of the mountain is an old, grumpy man who sleeps at the base of the mountain. If you wake him, you will suffer disaster on the mountain.

The Jos Plateau, located in the center of the country, was once the home of the Nok, an early culture that lived there from about 1000

Terracotta sculptures that were discovered in central Nigeria are some of the oldest in West Africa. These sculptures from the Nok people are estimated to have been created between 440 BCE and 200 CE.

BCE to 200 CE. The Nok are known for the terracotta sculptures of humans and animals that they left behind. Some are small, about the size that could be worn on a necklace. Others are life-size.

In the 19th century, groups of people with indigenous beliefs came to the plateau to escape the Muslim Fulani warriors. By then, Africans and the British had discovered tin and iron in the streams and rivers there. The plateau became one of the world's main suppliers of tin.

Although once forested, the Jos Plateau is now mainly grasslands. Goat and sheep herders have found another benefit to the Jos Plateau—because of the elevation, there are no tsetse flies there. These large flies, which are found only in Africa, carry a disease called trypanosomiasis. The disease is caused by a parasite that infects the central nervous system of humans and animals.

The sandy beaches and lagoons along Nigeria's coast provide places for visitors and residents to vacation. Nigeria's coastline runs approximately 530 miles (853 kilometers). The coast is humid all year long

Nigeria's beaches provide a quiet escape from the crowded cities.

with temperatures at their highest in the months of February and March.

Some people prefer the high heat to the dry season that begins around October. The North's dry season includes the dusty Harmattan wind, which can last up to four months.

The rainy season brings some relief. But like everything else, the amount of rain varies with the part of the country. Rains hit the South in March, but usually don't reach the North until May. The semi-desert in the far north part of the country may only get 50 inches (130 centimeters) or less of rain in a year. Yet along the coast, Nigeria receives approximately 150 inches (381 centimeters) annually.

Celebrations like the Durbar festival offer visitors a chance to see and experience traditional Nigerian culture.

Festival Time

Jeffrey Tayler, journalist and author of *Angry Wind* refers to Nigeria as the giant of Africa. "For millennia Nigeria's territory—a patchwork of Sahel, rain forest, and fertile plateau larger than Germany and France combined—has supported some of Africa's most advanced civilizations."[1]

The diversity of the land and the people carries over to a wide range of festivals and attractions, too. There's always something to do in Nigeria.

In the Muslim states in the North, Nigerians look forward to the Durbar, a huge festival that follows the Muslim holidays Eid-el-Fitr and Eid-el-Kabir. Various towns hold Durbars, but the most well-known is the Durbar in Kano which is attended by thousands of people.

Like many Nigerian festivals, the Durbar has a long history. In a traditional Durbar, the Emir, or Muslim leader of the village, watched as his military paraded on horseback. The modern Durbar in Kano still features a parade of horsemen, but today they are involved in races and mock fighting. Although the horsemen carry spears, swords, and clubs, most are fake.

In March, make your way to the banks of the Sokoto River where the Argungu Fishing and Cultural Festival lasts for four days. The festival isn't as old as some of Nigeria's other festivals, but it has grown since it began in 1934. The main attraction continues to be competitions in which fishermen wrestle fish from the river. Over time, canoe races and diving contests have also been added.

In Nigeria, yams are an important food source and also a reason for celebration.

For one of the most important Nigerian festivals, look to the yam, a starchy orange vegetable. Some people think yams and sweet potatoes are the same, but actually they come from different continents. Sweet potatoes are grown in North and South America; yams typically come from Africa and Asia. The yam is one of Nigeria's most important food crops, along with grains like rice, sorghum, tapioca, and millet.

The New Yam or Iri Ji Festival started long ago as a way to celebrate the harvest season. In preparation, old yams were eaten or tossed out. The first of the new yams were given to the king or chief of the village who would bless the harvest. Afterward, there would be lots of eating, everything made from yams.

In modern New Yam ceremonies, the yams are given to the oldest male in the village because Nigerians have a lot of respect for their elders. The elder offers the yams to the gods or ancestors. In many towns, the New Yam Festival signals the return of Nigerians to the villages they or their family come from. Together, people make improvements to the village during the time of the New Yam Festival.

Sometimes the New Yam Festival is incorporated into another festival. The Enugu State Masquerade Festival includes a New Yam ceremony. In this version, the head masquerader hands the yams to the governor.

Nigeria celebrates many holidays. Some of them are holidays that you might celebrate also—Christmas, New Year's, and Easter. Like the British, Nigerians also celebrate Boxing Day on the day after Christmas. In Britain, Boxing Day has been used to give a boxed gift to service providers, like the mail carrier. In Nigeria, Boxing Day is an excuse to head to the beach, the park, or a local event.

Boxing Day is also the beginning of Carnival Calabar in Nigeria, advertised as the largest cultural festival in Africa. Dances, parades, and music entertain Nigerians for two days. Crafts, drumming, food, and costume contests are also part of the celebration.

National Day on October 1 is an important holiday. It celebrates Nigeria's independence, just as Americans celebrate their independence on July 4. Ceremonies are usually held in Abuja at the Eagle Square parade grounds, but a car bombing at the 50th anniversary celebration in 2010 led to the 2011 celebration being moved to the more secure location of the president's villa. While a soldier sang "We Are the World," a military guard marched with flags and twirled its rifles. The ceremony ended with President Jonathan releasing a dove into the sky.

Many Nigerian families cannot afford the expense of a car. To get around, they use alternative means of transportation.

Chapter 6

The Culture of Nigeria

No matter what the size of the village or city, you might notice Nigerians in pairs or groups. Socializing or visiting with friends, family, and even strangers is a common occurrence in Nigeria. Family and friends are expected to stop by to visit without calling first.

To not greet another person is considered very bad manners. So if someone says good morning, good afternoon, or good evening—all used more commonly than "hello"—be sure to answer back. Ask how they are or how their family is and you're sure to get a big smile for your effort.

Family, including the extended family, is very important to Nigerians. Most families are led by a male. Polygamy—a man with more than one wife—is common in Nigeria. Although it mainly occurs in Muslim households, it sometimes happens in non-Muslim households as well. Women in non-Muslim homes have more freedom in clothing, working, and voicing their opinions.

Young people in cities may date, but dating is less common in North Nigeria and in rural areas. A man who wants to marry usually gives money, service, or property to the bride's family to formalize the marriage.

When a baby is born, it is cause for great celebration and naming ceremonies are held. Yoruba families name a child seven days after birth. Each parent and grandparent suggests a name, so some babies have many names. Igbo families may wait up to three months before holding a naming ceremony. A naming ceremony is usually accompanied by a feast of foods like smoked fish, yams, and kola nuts.

People in the South, in particular, are more outgoing. Loud voices are common, and many people enjoy a good debate. Don't worry if a Nigerian of the same gender as you seems to be standing too close while conversing; this is accepted social behavior.

You might notice some differences in the personalities of people in the North. They tend to speak with softer voices and are more conservative in their interactions with others. In addition, you're likely to see more conservative clothing in the Muslim states.

In the urban areas of the South, you might see people in t-shirts and jeans, but in other places, clothing is more traditional. Except for the North, clothing is often made from bright colors or bold patterns. Men wear loose, comfortable shirts with pants. You might see women in short-sleeve tops, wraparound skirts, and a scarf. Traditional Nigerian clothing is popular in other African countries, too.

It's rare to see people rushing off to appointments. Most people go about their daily life at a relaxed pace. There is time for everything that is important to the individual.

Even on days when there are no festivals or ceremonies, there is plenty to do in Nigeria. Sports are popular, particularly football. In the U.S., people know Nigeria's football as soccer.

The Super Eagles, Nigeria's national football team, have won many international championships. The team played its first official game in 1949 when Nigeria was still a British colony. It has gone on to play in four World Cup finals and even win a gold medal at the 1996 Olympics.

The members of the Nigeria national football team aren't the only gold-medal Nigerian athletes, and men aren't the only sports stars. Chioma Ajunwa was born on Christmas Day in 1970 in Umuihiokwu Mbaise, Imo State. She was the youngest of nine children. Her father died when she was only one year old, and her mother raised the children in poverty. Ajunwa enjoyed sports from a young age. Her mother tried to keep her from competing, but Ajunwa says she would climb out windows to get to a competition. Her mother finally gave up on changing her youngest child's mind.

When Ajunwa attended police training in Lagos, she was invited to the All-Africa Games championship being held in the city. She won the gold medal for the long jump. Five years before she competed in track and field at the 1996 Summer Olympics, she played soccer for the Nigerian women's team at the 1991 World Cup.

The 1996 Summer Olympics were held in Atlanta, Georgia. It can get fairly warm in the southern states during the summer, but Ajunwa was used to heat and humidity. At age twenty-five, she competed in three track and field events: a 4 x 100 relay, the 100 meters, and the long jump. She placed fifth in both the relay and the 100 meters. Although she made it to the semi-finals in the 100 meters, she wasn't able to match her personal best time of 10.84 seconds from 1992.

Only the long jump remained. When it was time for the finals, she ran toward the jump off point and launched her legs forward. She

Chioma Ajunwa is one of Nigeria's most famous athletes. She competed in three track and field events at the 1996 Olympics, winning a gold medal in the women's long jump.

jumped 7.12 meters in the first round. Chioma Ajunwa became the first Nigerian to win an individual Olympic gold medal and the first African woman to win an Olympic gold medal in a field event.

Did you know that a lot of music has roots in Nigeria? It may even be music that you listen to in the United States. People often refer to Nigerian music as world music, influencing other types of music like rhythm and blues and rap. Juju is a type of Nigerian music using the "talking drum." It doesn't really talk, but it has special tones that sound like words. Juju originated in the 1920s and was made popular in the 1960s and 70s by artists like Ebenezer Obey and King Sunny Adé.

All types of instruments are used in Nigerian music, but percussion instruments are favorites. There are different kinds of drums: pottery drums, cylinder drums, and slit-drums. Fuji music particularly uses

Nigeria's talking drums are not only popular in their native land, but around the world as well.

Nigeria has been participating in the Summer Olympics since 1952. In that time, Nigeria has won two gold medals, nine silver medals, and twelve bronze medals.

lots of drums. It comes from the music played during the call to prayer in the Muslim holy month of Ramadan. Musician Alhaji Sikiru Ayinde Barrister was the first to bring the sound to countries outside of Nigeria.

Call-and-response songs are part of the Nigerian musical heritage. In these songs, a chorus either repeats or answers a soloist. This type of song was also important in the development of American blues. Call-and-response songs are found in a type of Nigerian music known as Afrobeat. Popular since the 1960s, Afrobeat is a blend of jazz and funk. Like much of the popular music in Nigeria, people like to dance to Afrobeat.

Nigerian musician Fela Kuti is considered the father of Afrobeat. Fela Anikulapo Kuti was born in Abeokuta, Nigeria, in 1938 to Yoruban parents. He was a singer, composer, and bandleader who played the keyboard, trumpet, and saxophone. At the age of sixteen, he joined a popular band, the Cool Cats, and developed his own unique jazzy sound. By 1969, Kuti was sharing Afrobeat music with others, and went on a ten-month tour of the United States during which he was introduced to American jazz.

When Kuti returned to Africa, he changed the name of his band to Africa '70. The band featured many singers, dancers, and musicians. Instruments in the popular Afrobeat band included drums and other percussion instruments, guitars, saxophones, and trumpets.

In addition to being an outstanding musician, Kuti was very outspoken about Nigeria's political issues. He often criticized the Nigerian government. In 1979, he created his own political party, MOP (Movement of the People). When the military took over the government in 1983, Kuti was one of the many people arrested. Falsely charged with smuggling money, Kuti was released in 1986.

Fela Kuti, one of Nigeria's most popular musicians, died in 1997 of complications from AIDS.

Abuja became Nigeria's capital in 1991.
Almost two million people live in the city.

The Cities of Nigeria

Abuja, Nigeria's capital, is a city of approximately 1.8 million people, located in the ethnically neutral center of the country. But Abjua wasn't always the capital. The busy port city of Lagos was Nigeria's capital from colonial days until 1991. The largest city in Nigeria and the second-largest in Africa after Cairo, Egypt, the streets of Lagos are crowded with people walking and driving. Lagos has over five times as many people as Abuja. With 10 million people, Lagos can be overwhelming for visitors.

Lagos lies next to the Gulf of Guinea, part of the Atlantic Ocean. During colonialism, the Portuguese, and later the British, used the port at Lagos for shipping. It has been Nigeria's most important city since its days as a Yoruba port city and a British center of power. According to author Richard Dowden, "Lagos is the heart of Nigeria and its gateway to the world."[1]

The center of commercial activity in the city is Lagos Island, which began as the fishing village, Eko. When former slaves were freed from Brazil, many of them returned to the island and built homes similar to the ones they had found in Brazil. Today, Brazilian-style buildings are plentiful on Lagos Island.

The city of Lagos includes Lagos Island, neighboring islands, and the mainland. Bridges connect the mainland with Lagos Island and Victoria Island. Between the islands and the mainland is Lagos Lagoon.

The Lekki Market is a hidden gem in Lagos that offers crafts and other Nigerian treasures. For tourists willing to barter, it can be a great place to find souvenirs.

There is much to do in Lagos. The Lekki Market includes ancient Nigerian art and sculptures. Mosques and cathedrals stand as majestic examples of the city's architecture. In Badagry, a section of the state of Lagos, you will find signs of Badagry's history as a slave port. Slave chains, holding cells, and wharfs where slaves were shipped are preserved here. Badagry was one of the first slavery ports in West Africa, dating back to the early 1500s. Over half a million Africans were sent to other countries as slaves from this port.

Officials often recommend that tourists do not use credit cards or traveler's checks in Nigeria because fraud is common. Instead, visitors have to exchange their money for Nigerian naira. Moneychangers are found in the streets in certain parts of the city.

When you are hungry, there are plenty of places to find "chop," or food, in Nigeria. Favorite native dishes have a peppery taste and smell. Jollof is a peppery rice, and pepper stew is popular too. Pepper stew has more than just pepper in it. It usually includes meat and vegetables, as well. Rice dishes are popular because rice is grown locally and is easily combined with other ingredients. Tuwo are balls made of rice or other grains. They are popular in the North, and typically eaten with soup or sauce. Yoruba foods tend to be spicier than the foods of other ethnic groups.

Fruits are readily available in Nigeria. Bananas, oranges, guavas, pineapples, and papayas make good snacks. Raw sugar cane is a sweet treat.

You might notice that Nigerians almost always eat with their right hand. Passing something to another person is either done with both hands or only the right hand, but never just the left hand. The left hand is considered unclean.

Even though Lagos is a modern city, people still use wood and charcoal for cooking, and much of the city gets its water from a vertical pipe called a standpipe. Electricity is erratic and may go off at any time.

Many people live in apartments in the cities. Single family homes may be constructed from cement blocks with a wood or metal sheet roof. In the country, many houses are built with handmade mud bricks dried in the sun. Roofs are made from branches or palm leaves. Indoor bathrooms are much more common in cities than in rural areas.

The state of Lagos contains a large amount of water in lagoons, rivers, and creeks. This and the abundant rainfall contribute to the wetlands and tropical swamp forests. Lagos is the smallest state in Nigeria, but it holds the largest number of people.

The traffic is almost always heavy in Lagos. Many of Nigeria's roads are busy with cars, and not all of these roads are paved. Most people take a bus or a bush taxi to get to another city. A bush taxi is a large cab or minibus that is often crowded with people. Bush taxis run on their own schedules, which usually means no schedule.

Northeast of Lagos is the city of Osogbo, the home of fine Nigerian contemporary art and markets. Perhaps Osogbo's biggest draw is the Osun Sacred Forest, also known as the Osun-Osogbo Sacred Grove, on the outskirts of the city. Named a UNESCO World Heritage Site in 2005, the thick, green forest is a shrine to Yoruba gods and the home to Osun, the goddess of fertility. The forest contains palaces, sculptures, and prayer sites. At one time, each Yoruba village established a sacred grove nearby, however this may be the only one that remains today.

Kano is one of the oldest cities in West Africa, founded over a thousand years ago at the crossroads of a trans-Saharan trade route. Forest people traded ivory, kola nuts, and slaves for salt, cloth, weapons, coral, and glass beads from the Berbers of North Africa.

Today, Kano is Nigeria's second-largest city after Lagos. It is also the home of the Kurmi Market, one of Africa's largest markets, where visitors can find fine metal crafts, statues, and jewelry. You can also buy leather items, native instruments, and ostrich feather shoes! Be prepared to bargain—it's part of the experience.

Also in Kano are the Kofar Mata Dye Pits, where indigo cloth has been dyed for hundreds of years. The Gidan Makama Museum, formerly a king's palace from the 15th century, features the traditional mud-walled Hausan architecture.

In addition to Hausa kingdoms, Nigeria had other ancient kingdoms as well. The kingdom of Oyo was located in the southwestern part of

Kofar Mata Dye Pits

The Gidan Makama Museum

the country. Founded in the 14th century, Oyo was a political center for West Africa from the 1600s to the 1800s. The kingdom of Benin, located to the south of Oyo, was established in 1440. With a well-trained army, Benin also boasted a sophisticated ceremonial court decorated with works of art in bronze, ivory, and wood.

Before the kingdom of Benin was established in Benin City, artists created sculptures from brass, possibly as early as the 13th century. Brass statuary was one of the first African arts to be recognized throughout the world. Craftsmen continue to work on brass sculptures, but to see how the statues have changed over the years, check out the National Museum of Benin City.

While Nigeria is known for its brass sculptures, they aren't the only art form you'll see. Artisans also like to carve from wood and soap-stone. The wood masks seen at cultural festivals are works of art you won't find anywhere else. Other artists paint to celebrate Nigeria's tribal culture.

Nigerian President Goodluck Jonathan met with U.S. President Barack Obama at the White House on June 8, 2011. The leaders discussed working together to strengthen the partnership between their two countries.

A Land of Possibilities

When Nigeria became independent, it sought a greater unity with other African nations. Nigeria enjoys good relationships with its immediate neighbors, except for a border dispute with Cameroon that was resolved in 2008. As a member of the United Nations, Nigeria supports African peacekeeping missions. The country has provided most of the troops for UN missions in Liberia, Sudan, and Sierra Leone.

Although the United States had once imposed sanctions against Nigeria due to criminal government actions, those days are now over. U.S. Secretary of State Hillary Clinton made Nigeria part of her first official visit to Africa in 2009. This led to the establishment of the U.S.-Nigeria Binational Commission the following year. The commission focuses on talks between the two countries about government, security, the Niger Delta, energy, investment, and agriculture.

President Jonathan visited the White House on June 8, 2011 and met with President Barack Obama. Jonathan was in the United States to participate in a United Nations HIV/AIDS meeting.

It's estimated that over 250,000 Nigerians live in the United States. Some relocated for work, and many attend universities. Approximately 25,000 Americans currently live in Nigeria. Many work in the petroleum industry.

Health care is one area that Nigeria hopes to improve during the coming years. The life expectancy in Nigeria is currently 52.05 years. Compare that to the United States at 78.49 years, or Monaco at 89.68

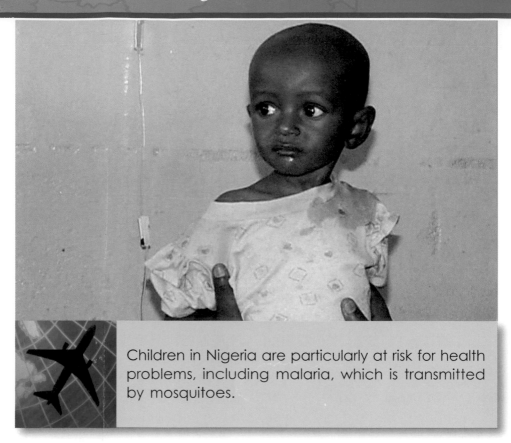

Children in Nigeria are particularly at risk for health problems, including malaria, which is transmitted by mosquitoes.

years. The death rate for mothers and infants is significant. About two-thirds of births take place in homes and most have no health care provider present. Childbirth and child malaria lead to the deaths of over 300,000 children each year.

Diseases that hit Nigeria hardest are AIDS and tuberculosis (TB). Nigeria has the second-largest population of people with HIV in the world, over three million. The only country with more people infected with HIV is South Africa. Nigeria leads Africa in TB, a contagious disease that affects the lungs.

The infectious disease rate is high and includes hepatitis, typhoid fever, yellow fever, and malaria. Improvements in the water supply are helping to slow the spread of disease. Three-quarters of urban areas have safe water sources, but that rate falls to 42 percent in rural areas. Eliminating diseases like malaria and yellow fever, which are transmitted by insects, is another of Nigeria's goals.

In May of 2011, the United Nations congratulated the Nigerian government for their health initiatives for maternal and child health. Officials have combined maternal/child health services with programs on nutrition, tuberculosis, and HIV.

Nigeria's education system needs improvements, as well. Among people fifteen and older, 61 percent can read and write. This is about the same percentage of the population that attends primary school. Only about half of those continue to high school. The average student stays in school for five years, with boys more likely to go on to secondary schools than girls.

That's not always the case, however. Dr. Bene Madunagu is a Nigerian woman with a great deal of education. As a biologist, she heads the botany department at the University of Calabar in Nigeria.

Slightly over half of Nigerian children attend school, but their government aims to improve enrollment rates in the near future.

Wearing t-shirts that read "Ask me About Reproductive Health," members of a human rights club help educate fellow female students in Enugu State, Nigeria.

She spends much of her time encouraging young Nigerian women to educate themselves and fighting for women's equality.

She helped create Women in Nigeria (WIN), an organization that works for equal rights. Then, in 1993, she and Grace Osakue founded Girls' Power Initiative, a program to provide health education and counseling for girls between ten and eighteen years of age. Girls' Power Initiative later won awards from the MacArthur Foundation Fund for Leadership Development and Creative & Effective Institutions.

Dr. Madunagu was chosen as the General Coordinator of DAWN (Development Alternatives with Women for a New Era) in 2003. DAWN is a group of female scholars who work for women's interests.

In rural areas in particular, young children may not know English, yet schools often are taught in English. This sets students up for failure in school at a very early age. Some people are trying to change this by providing primary schools taught in the first languages of Nigeria's children.

In the Nigerian states that follow Islamic law, boys and girls go to separate schools. These schools also focus largely on religious studies.

Improvements are taking place all the time in Nigeria. Civilian democratic government has lasted more than ten years. Already one of the largest economies in Africa, many people believe Nigeria's economy has a lot of potential to grow even larger with proper planning and management. Nigeria's national motto is "Unity and Faith, Peace and Progress." It is a good motto for a proud nation.

The sun rises over Nigeria

Nigerian Recipe

Boiled Yams

Yams are a very important food in Nigeria. They are used in festivals and for everyday meals. Yams are often served with stew, or even eggs.

Ingredients:
4 Yams (one per person)
Water
2 tsp. Salt

1. **With adult supervision,** peel the skins off the yams with a knife.
2. Rinse the yams.
3. Cut the yams into 1-inch (2.5 centimeters) wide slices.
4. Place the slices in a pot and add enough water to cover them.
5. Add salt.
6. Bring the water to a boil, and cook over medium heat for 15-30 minutes. After 15 minutes, check every 5 minutes to see if they are ready. Yams are ready when a fork goes through them easily.
7. Drain the yams.

Nigerian Craft — Talking Drum

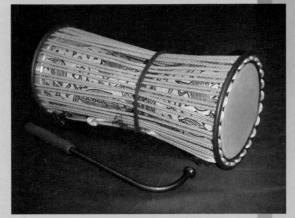

Supplies
2 plastic flowerpots
Stretchy fabric, such as polyester
Marker or fabric pen
Ruler
Scissors
Plastic ties
Duct tape
String
Glue
Paint
Paint brush
Wooden spoon

1. Set the top of a planter on the fabric. Trace around the edge of the pot with the marker.
2. Measure two inches out from the first circle and draw another circle.
3. Between the two circles, draw dots all the way around, about two inches apart from each other.
4. Cut out the outer circle.
5. With the scissors, poke holes where the dots are.
6. Repeat steps 1 through 5 with the second planter, making sure both circles have the same number of holes.
7. Tie the small ends of the two pots together with plastic ties or something similar. Wrap duct tape around the area where the two pots connect.
8. Place each fabric circle at either end.
9. Tie one end of a long piece of string to a hole in the material. Run the string to a hole at the other end. Continue going back and forth from one end to the other as you go around the drum until the string goes through all the holes. Pull the string tight and tie it to the last hole.
10. Mix equal amounts of glue and water together and paint one of the fabric ends of the drum. Let it dry and repeat on the other side.
11. Decorate the fabric ends of the drum with paint.
12. Use a plastic or wooden spoon as a drumstick. Hold the drum under one arm, and play the drum by pressing on different strings or holding the drum in different positions for different pitches.

1000-1300	Hausa and Yoruba cultures are major powers in areas now known as Nigeria.
1472	Portuguese arrive in Nigeria.
1700s	Britain, Portugal, and the Netherlands dominate slave trade along Nigerian coast; severe drought and famine in Sahel.
1804-1810	Fulani War; Islam spreads among the Hausa.
1851	British occupy Lagos.
1859	First Nigerian newspaper is published.
1861	Lagos becomes a British territory.
1872	First prison established in Nigeria.
1886	British rule has spread to the Yoruba; charter granted to the National African Company (later called the Royal Niger Company) for trade along the Niger River.
1900	Britain expands its control to all of Nigeria.
1914	Britain's control is formalized when Nigeria is named the Colony and Protectorate of Nigeria.
1915	First commercial coal mine opens in the town of Enugu.
1933	Lagos Youth Movement is established, later known as the Nigerian Youth Movement.
1949	*Nigerian Tribune* newspaper is first published.
1955	First women recruited into the Nigeria Police Force.
1956	Oil discovered by Shell Darcy at Oloibiri in the Niger Delta.
1960	On October 1, Nigeria achieves independence from Britain.
1966	Nigerian military holds its first coup and takes over the government.
1967	Igbo form the Republic of Biafra; civil war begins.
1970	Civil war between Nigeria and Biafra ends with over a million dead, Republic of Biafra dissolved.
1976	Seven new states added to Nigeria, for a total of nineteen.
1979	Second Republic of Nigeria is established, with a civilian government; Alhaji Shehu Shagari of the National Party of Nigeria wins the presidential election.
1981-1983	World oil market glut causes economic problems for Nigeria.
1981	Minimum wage is introduced in Nigeria with the National Minimum Wage Act.

1983	Border disputes arise between Nigeria and Cameroon; Shagari is reelected president of Nigeria, but is overthrown by Major General Muhammadu Buhari before the end of the year.
1987	Government increases the number of states in Nigeria to twenty-one.
1991	Nine more states are added, bringing the total to thirty.
1992	Nigeria's GDP is $25 billion, the second-highest in Africa, but the average income is only $267 a year.
1993	Presidential election projects M.K.O. Abiola to win in June; General Babangida annuls the election and throws Abiola in prison; General Sani Abacha takes over the Nigerian government and abolishes the constitution.
1995	Military government executes many political activists who oppose the government, including writer Ken Saro-Wiwa.
1998	General Sani Abacha dies of a heart attack in June.
1999	Olusegun Obasanjo sworn in as president of Third Republic of Nigeria.
2010	A car bomb goes off at National Day festivities on October 1, killing at least seven people.
2011	Goodluck Jonathan is reelected president with 59 percent of the vote.
2012	Hundreds are killed in attacks by the terrorist group Boko Haram throughout the year.

CHAPTER NOTES

Chapter Notes
Chapter 3. The Journey of Democracy
1. Goodluck Jonathan, *Facebook* (Fan page),
    http://www.facebook.com/jonathangoodluck
Chapter 5. Festival Time
1. Jeffrey Tayler, *Angry Wind* (Boston: Houghton Mifflin Co., 2005), p. 107.
Chapter 7. The Cities of Nigeria
1. Richard Dowden, *Africa: Altered States, Ordinary Miracles* (Great Britain: Portobello Books, 2009), p. 439.

Bewer, Tim, et. al. *Lonely Planet West Africa.* Oakland, CA: Lonely Planet, 2009.

Carnival Calabar. http://www.carnivalcalabar.com/about/carnival

CultureGrams World Edition 2010: Africa. ProQuest LLC/Brigham Young University, 2009.

Dowden, Richard. *Africa: Altered States, Ordinary Miracles.* Great Britain: Portobello Books, 2009.

Falola, Toyin. *Culture & Customs of Nigeria.* Westport, CT: Greenwood Publishing Group, Inc., 2000.

Freeman, Joel A. "Badagry, Nigeria: Their History in the Atlantic Slave Trade." The Freeman Institute. http://www.freemaninstitute.com/Gallery/nigeria.htm

Ham, Anthony, et. al. *Africa.* Oakland, CA: Lonely Planet, 2010.

Insight into Igbo Culture, Igbo Language, and Enugu. http://www.igboguide.org/

Jonathan, Goodluck. *Facebook* (Fan page). http://www.facebook.com/jonathangoodluck

"Masks And Masquerades of Oraifite Igbo Land." Oraifite Community Town. http://www.oraifite.com/masks-and-masquerades

McColl, R.W., Ph.D, Editor. *Encyclopedia of World Geography,* (Volume 2). New York: Facts on File, Inc., 2005.

Motherland Nigeria. http://www.motherlandnigeria.com

"Nigeria: Chronology Of The Struggle For Stability And Democracy." All Africa, August 24, 2000. http://allafrica.com/stories/200008240352.html

Nigeria's 50th Independence Anniversary. http://nigeriaat50.gov.ng/

"Nigeria." U.S. Department of State. http://www.state.gov/r/pa/ei/bgn/2836.htm

Nok Culture. http://nokculture.com/

Online Nigeria. http://www.onlinenigeria.com

Tayler, Jeffery. *Angry Wind.* Boston: Houghton Mifflin Co., 2005.

Williams, Lizzie. *Nigeria.* Chalfont St Peter, Great Britain: Bradt Travel Guides, 2008.

FURTHER READING

Books

Achebe, Chinua. *Chike and the River.* New York: Anchor Books, 1966.

Bojang, Ali Brownlie. *Discover Nigeria.* New York: Powerkids Press, 2011.

Giles, Bridget. *Nigeria.* Washington, D.C.: National Geographic, 2007.

Heinrichs, Ann. *Nigeria: Enchantment of the World.* New York: Children's Press, 2009.

Murphy, Patricia J. *Nigeria.* Salt Lake City: Benchmark Books/Marshall Cavendish, 2005.

Okegbenro, Bernae. *The Naming Ceremony.* Atlanta: Enrichment Reading, 2008.

Oluonye, Mary N. *Nigeria.* Minneapolis: Lerner Publications Co., 2008.

Onyefulu, Ifeoma. *An African Christmas.* Great Britain: Frances Lincoln Limited, 2005.

On the Internet

"Africa." PBS.
    http://www.pbs.org/wnet/africa/index.html

Gates, Henry Louis, Jr. "Wonders of the African World." PBS.
    http://www.pbs.org/wonders/

"The Gashaka Primate Project." Gashaka-Gumti National Park, Nigeria, and Department of Anthropology, University College, London.
    http://www.ucl.ac.uk/gashaka/home/

United States Diplomatic Mission to Nigeria.
    http://nigeria.usembassy.gov/

Visiting Nigeria.
    http://www.visitingnigeria.com/

GLOSSARY

agriculture (AG-ruh-kul-chur): farming

coup (KOO): a sudden takeover of power by force

culture (KUHL-chur): the traditions and customs of a group of people

ethnicity (ETH-nis-i-tee): racial or cultural background

export (EK-sport): to sell products to another country or the product being sold to another country

hominid (HAH-muh-nid): the classification of primates that stand and move on two feet, such as humans, gorillas, and chimpanzees

import (IM-port): to bring a products into a country or the product being brought in to a country

indigenous (in-DIJ-uh-nus): native

lagoon (luh-GOON): a shallow pool of seawater separated from the ocean by a narrow strip of land

masquerade (mass-kuh-RADE): an event where people dress in costume or disguise themselves

parliament (PAR-luh-muhnt): a group of people that have been elected to make laws in some countries

plateau (pla-TOH): an area of high, flat land

republic (ri-PUHB-lik): a form of government in which the people have power to elect officials

savanna (suh-VAN-nuh): a tropical or subtropical grassland with scattered trees and seasonal rainfall

shari'a (shuh-REE-uh): code of law based on the sacred book of Islam, the Koran

statuary (STATCH-oo-er-ee): statues

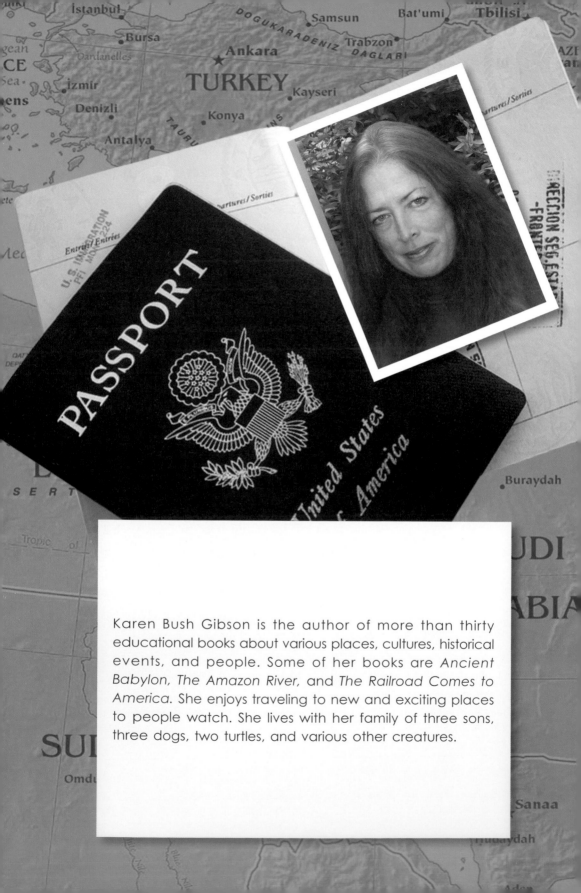

Karen Bush Gibson is the author of more than thirty educational books about various places, cultures, historical events, and people. Some of her books are *Ancient Babylon*, *The Amazon River*, and *The Railroad Comes to America*. She enjoys traveling to new and exciting places to people watch. She lives with her family of three sons, three dogs, two turtles, and various other creatures.